Every Child Is Beautiful When Born
Selected Poems

Esad Babačić

EVERY CHILD IS BEAUTIFUL WHEN BORN
SELECTED POEMS

Translated from the Slovenian by Andrej Pleterski

DALKEY ARCHIVE PRESS
Dallas / Dublin

ISBN: 978-1-628973-40-2

Library of Congress Cataloging-in-Publication Data available upon request.

Published in cooperation with the Slovene Writers' Association— Litterae Slovenicae Series.

This book was published with the support of Trubar Foundation at the Slovene Writers' Association, Ljubljana, Slovenia.

This translation has been financially supported by the Slovenian Book Agency and the European Commission.

www.dalkeyarchive.com

Dallas / Dublin

Printed on permanent/durable acid-free paper

Every Child Is Beautiful When Born
Selected Poems

Esad Babačić

WHAT A POEM NEEDS

Air.
Plenty of air.
And a landscape.
A human in the middle,
sitting by the fire,
warming his hands.

(*Whales Do Not Showboat*, 2000)

A NATIVE AMERICAN POEM

I'd like to live with a sky
that will devour me.

(*Cut Off from the Sky*, 2018)

EVERY CHILD IS BEAUTIFUL WHEN BORN

At first, you want to go out to count the stars.
The shadow is slow, it doesn't catch
your thoughts.

Once you know how to run, you never give up,
once you know how to run, you attempt suicide.

If you were still alive, you'd laugh for a long time.
You're only beautiful when born.

Don't look out the window,
you may not feel like living just then,
and jump down.

Every child is beautiful when born.

(*Born Before My Mother I'd Be Free*, fanzine, 1982)

THE RETREAT

One of those days
with nobody taking defense
because nobody's making an attack.
With the stadiums empty
and a draw,
the best score for all.
With ropes lowered down
below the knees
and belts hanging
on the doors
someone forgot to close,
not caring at all.
With the emptiness
returning to the suburb.
With the traffic light flashing for itself.
With curtains making love with windows
and the poor seeking power.
With you only sitting in the corner,
looking for the root of the word
silence.

(*Cut Off from the Sky*, 2018)

THE DANUBE

The footsteps grow out into infinity,
the abandonment resounds into yet another
reason. Once I open up completely, an explosion
will probably occur, whereby the last hope

might fly off, a world more transparent
than the origin of thinking. The power grows
from the mind, it's unstoppable, it's going to be
aggressive again, like so many times before.

What if I tell them *no*, what if I don't
have mercy on the power? Will it sail off,
leaving some more emptiness for new
desires—will the slow contracting of disease

gain momentum, will the souls stop
the blind bobbing across the steppes
of the lost nation? The hectic movement
of the man on the verge of the mature age

and now an already healthy attitude to the fact
that sometimes one is unable to move on,
that a silent reference point can stand still, that
joy can find no motivation. And why the babbling

of the Danubian birds speaks volumes about
your endless unrest. Let yourself be surprised
by the angel of devastation one more time,
and you'll come to realize there had been
no reason, no reason whatsoever.

(*Whales Do Not Showboat*, 2000)

THE OUTER STARS

The death of some people
is so sad
it is never
spoken about anymore.
We just remain silent,
afraid of it
being repeated,
until, one day,
the sadness is replaced
by fury,
one big crystal
made of unshed tears,
the fury we did not
cry more
when necessary,
the fury we
had to smile
just for show
and forget
about the grace
that remains alone

with those
that are still
out there, beyond
the silence of stars . . .

(*Cut Off from the Sky*, 2018)

TO THE SOLDIER OF SILENCE

You know well what kills you.
Then you go there
and start doing it.
In the evening, you keep
returning to the dark
of your room,
and look back:
mistakes, golden mistakes.

(*The Wind in the Veins*, 1994)

THE WIND

I

The head always needs to be open on one side.
For birds to fly.
For waters to run.
For things to die.
The head always needs to be open on one side.
For the wind to awaken us again from behind.

II

For the wind to awaken us again from behind,
you need to have a hole from the bullet.
Or else it doesn't pay off.
The waters stand still.
And the birds cannot fly.

(*The Angel with Shredded Wings*, 1989)

THE DAY

I knew it.
You'd walk, growing ever smaller,
with the crowd ever bigger.

(*Cut Off from the Sky*, 2018)

ARARAT

I'm about to turn forty and I still lie to myself and others.
I tell jokes about life, preferably the one about the mountain.
At about thirty, you still feel you're climbing up, and then,
on suddenly reaching the peak, you look down, appalled,
wipe off your forehead and start descending. I'm descending.

I'm not always sure whether it's a good or a bad thing,
I just notice it's all the same for the mountain, the only one
to know I've only seen her from one side never to reach
its peak. All she can leave me is the illusion I live with.

The mountain is my patron saint, the only convincing lie.
When I no longer see her one day, I won't know
it's too late. So, I don't have to fear now.
It's eight A.M., Jože got up long ago and
went out to seek the right light.
It's time I headed for the other side
unless I want to become an old liar
like so many in this town.
Sorry I'm late.
But isn't it all the same?

(*The Divan*, 2006)

B. B.[1]

Hey, my friend, I've ended up in a museum of modern art.
You'd surely say: better this than being dead. Maybe yes.
I now invite all my friends who forgot me, anyone still alive,
to come to visit me. The entrance fee, three euros. And fifty cents.
You can enter for free, though, I know you haven't got this much.
Just tell the receptionist you've come to see me.
We'll have a word about the longing that's gone,
about the melancholy everyone resents till it's too late,
about the depression nobody wants 'cause it can't be cured.
But, dude, you know, you need to have the balls
for depression too, you have to care less than her.
You just mustn't look back, like when you ski.
Everything's white and you're white till you see your own blood.
Although, here, everything is turned backward.
The tomb of time, ideas, victories, and defeats.
The cool light of the world I switch on
and off, every day, before and after work.
Look, do stop by if you want, if you're not so cynical and
self-satisfied anymore. You know it, the day comes
when this doesn't help anymore. You rot away. Fall out. Greater

---

[1] Brane Bitenc (1962–2014), the singer of the cult punk band "Otroci socializma" (The
Children of Socialism) (1981–1986), a poet, and a film producer, who committed suicide.

cynics will come, the muscular masters of quarrel and pounce.
You're just a knight whose sword keeps getting stuck.
And the mirror's no longer a shield, but an illusion, a
deception,
a hand of a failed underhandedness. I won't beg you,
I've got my pride though you don't give a shit about it.
But at least you don't pretend it means something to you.
Indeed, this is what had actually killed us:
we started to pretend as though we cared.
And they got us, for next to nothing.
Every revolution ends up in a museum, sooner or later.
And I like it, you know, that Coca-Cola is here too,
that it got locked up too, as an exhibit
of human folly and progress.
It's ended up in here,
but still they drink it because they can't stop.
There're so many more things I'd lock in here.
The blood, yours, mine, the cold gazes and the warm embraces,
the walls that cry without us, the empty streets on Sundays,
the flags that don't flipping care, the bells that bang to no avail,
and the courage of the suicides we're not supposed
to cry for.

(*Kitula*, 2015)

THE MELANCHOLY

You keep choosing me.
Over and over.
You lay the cards
and close your eyes.
You know well
what I'll pick and
how much I'll leave out.
You don't care,
less than myself,
and this keeps you
afloat.
I'm the one
who's sinking and
being hooked
by the plankton of the night.
Every spark from the depths
pulls me into itself.
I trust you too much
and give too little
for you to be able
to knock me to the bottom.
As long as it's like this,

I remain your slave,
a melancholic brother,
the prisoner of a golden boat
pushing its way into the muddy eternity.

(*Kitula*, 2015)

THE PRESSURE

I walk from wall to wall.
And my head aches from you.
Why don't I crash at all?
Into a wall.
Into a wall.

(*Black Jack*, 1994)

A PROPER POEM

You've lived properly,
properly will you die.
You've had proper relationships
with proper people
in the proper times.
You've been a proper example
of properness.
You've remained proper
in your fear
even when everybody
took their
share of improperness
and rejoiced
improperly.
Once you even lied
to yourself
that yourself too
could easily be
improper at times,
just to stay proper
till the end.
Today you admitted
properly to being guilty
that the bad guys

had won, and of being
properly naive too
in feeding them with your
properness
because you didn't know
properness
had always been
the greatest
asset held
by the most
improper
people.

(*Kitula*, 2015)

A NAIVE POEM

You were good,
too good.
And everybody
would like you
as long as you were
like this,
pleasing
them in everything,
turning the cheek
twice
when
somebody
lost control
accidentally.
All
you had
was
never to
believe
anybody,
and the pride
you would
hide
carefully.

As long as you
were kind
to them,
they would let
you be,
but the first time
you didn't
please
them,
they told you
to be
grateful
they let
you be
good,
too good.

(*Arrivals, Departures*, 2013)

TRIESTE

It's hard for me to be a poet
in this city of plastic bags.
When I started writing, I hoped
I'd fled them.
By the evening, the heavy roller shutters
had blocked the view of the shop windows.
I had a good cry and the bag
seemed lighter, at least at that point.
What a pity they didn't notice it.
All they saw in me were
the shoes and the cheap briefs.
No protection for me in that city
that should have belonged to us.
I'm here today, bagless,
I read poems and I have a name.
But anyway: give me back my bags,
give me back my tears I'd hide
so skillfully in them
when buying the shoes,
the cheap briefs,
and those packages
with fragrant butterflies.

(*Whales Do Not Showboat*, 2000)

JLA

The inscription on my military service book.
I didn't know how to wait.
The JLA was a flock of happy hostages
never to be shot.
The Titograd heat,
the last three hundred
meters of peace,
and Morrison;
seven miles
ride the snake.

The gods of the unhappy
are too gentle.
Get to know them, soldier.

First, you need to destroy
yourself. Then starts
the agony of love
and longing for what you are
never to accomplish.

Because it's too late
for you to like what
you've never liked.
And to understand
what you never could.

And so you pity the gods
that keep coming down
to help us.

(*Cut Off from the Sky*, 2018)

WHAT ELSE?

What else
will you take from me?
The joy
that chases
sadness.
The laughter
that runs away
from tears.
The emptiness
larger
than pride.
The pride
that keeps me
afloat.
The mountain
I stand on.
And the sun
I like to gaze into.
What else
will you take from me?
The rivers
under my feet
and the shoes
under my heels.

The eternal circle
I enchanted
with my birth.
And the end
I play with
in the evening.
I wish to be
alone again,
without your
departures,
without
your delusions.

(*Arrivals, Departures*, 2013)

RAIN

It rains here all the time.
The dirty windows,
the dirty people,
the endless thicket
of the conquering trash
hiding
in the glass
castles of self-conceit.

(*Elephants Have a Fair Cry*, 2011)

We all drown
with hair
in our hands.

(*Arrivals, Departures*, 2013)

A REVOLUTION

Yesterday,
a revolution took place.
Yesterday, we screamed at each other
with greater care than usual.
Yesterday, I got
the fastest car in the village.
A Croatian general
was sentenced
to 40 years in jail,
we were sentenced
to standing in lines at shopping malls
for thousands of years.

(*Elephants Have a Fair Cry*, 2011)

DEMOCRACY

Democracy is when your phone rings
and you pick up the receiver
with nobody on the other side.
Democracy is when the entire skyscraper cannot sleep
because of a hungry dog barking beneath the window,
locked in a cage by his owner.
Democracy is when you call
the SPCA
as you can no longer
listen to the desperate dog,
and they tell you
there's nothing they can do—
once the laws are adopted . . .
once it becomes legal . . .
we'll bark too.
Democracy is when somebody
previously poor
remains poor in the future.

(*Black Jack*, 1994)

THE PARTISAN POEM

As kids, we'd play
Germans and Partisans.

I was always a German,
which annoyed me.

When I came home one day,
I complained to my mother
I wanted to be a Partisan.
She told me not to
ever open the door to anybody
and to always stay at home.
If you stay at home,
you won't play
Germans and Partisans anymore,
you'll eat more
and at least gain some weight.

That seemed like a good idea.
I might really gain some weight,
I thought to myself. And then I'd
be strong enough to always
be a Partisan.

My friends would knock on our door,
and I wouldn't answer.
Years would pass by and I'd eat,
cry, and gain weight.

And when I no longer felt like a kid,
I decided to join
the Partisans again.

One day
I wrote a letter to my mother
on a piece of paper, telling her I was
going to the woods to become a Partisan.

I'd only wait for her
to read it
and then escape.
But it wasn't to happen.
Because my mother couldn't read.
Socialism didn't teach
her this.

I felt the war,
the power and the powerlessness of Germans,
and I still feel it today.

I never wanted to be a German,
but my mother kept telling me
to stay at home, at least
to gain some weight.

I've always wanted to be a Partisan,
but what can I do if my mother can't read,
socialism didn't teach her this.

(*Black Jack*, 1994)

A MACEDONIAN POEM

You try hard.
Each bill paid by the first day of month.
The light in the room fears
your bloodstream might freeze.
You write home
every Christmas
even though you don't celebrate it.
You build skyscrapers
you'll never live in,
stadiums where
you'll never cheer for anybody,
hotels to be slept in by
those who snub you.
You try not to be
too visible
in order for them
not to see
your anguish.
Only with the doctor
can you share
your suffering,
how you wake up in the night,
screaming both at yourself
for trying so hard

and your kids
for having listened to you.
You built roads
and houses for those
you trusted, and now
you keep moving out of their way
when they try to run over you.
For being too slow.

Each bill paid by the first day of month,
each duty carried out,
toward yourself and the world.
Because you're never late
even though you know everything is late.
Death is late
and this damn peace is late too.
Roses are falling from the sky,
heavy, white roses,
instead of rain.

(*Arrivals, Departures*, 2013)

A GREEN LAND

There's a manic
depression of economy,
a psychosis of taking away
heartlessly,
a manic depression
of constructive engineering,
a depression of graves
never in short supply.
Permits are growing,
published as books,
we walk on prescriptions,
lifting them up
like unread skyscrapers,
the steel visions
of our highs
and lows.
We walk on the statistics,
not the roads,
not the rain,
we march on the clouds,
on the clouds
traveling faster
because they've come
from afar.

They are pushed by
Chinese underpeople
with their heads bent,
eyes shut, licking, counting,
the project leaders of stable markets,
in the vacuum of ongoing
decision-making.
Every fix you act out
is doomed to victory
or defeat,
yet it's no longer our choice,
there's no choice for us anymore,
just the hands,
the rubber hands
of the autumn depression
freed from steel,
wanting to
suck us into itself,
into the psychosis of desire
and command.

Your heart
is a green
land
punished
with beauty.

(*Kitula*, 2015)

A GLASS LAND

The trees,
headless.
The trees,
hairless.
The trees
of our misery,
our headless
temptations.
The trees
falling
within us
not to ever
pick ourselves up
not to ever
rise again.
The trees,
we want more.
We want to go over there,
to the other side
of the eternal mountain.
Your
white
and bare
mountain.

Without you,
we'll walk
on it
and weep,
bent
to the ground,
having been too late
to see.
Having regarded you
only
as beauty
we were not
able to tell
much
about.

(*Kitula*, 2015)

ĐIĐIKOVAC

To Ahmed Burić

The sleeves of the old sweater
have never been long enough
to cover up the slender wrists,
always ready for that
typical move,
an enigmatic curve
similar to that turn from the childhood
where it struck you for the first time
you'd be climbing
this hill deep into the old age.
Believing is the slowest
balsam of aging.
No shortcuts
even though you need to run at times
to trick the chatter of the charshia.
Refilling coffee cups is a prolongation of moments
that aren't talked about.

The tapping of the fildan
remains the first and the final prayer
of the Sarajevo elevations
you're no longer supposed to dream about.

(*Whales Do Not Showboat*, 2000)

ARRIVALS, DEPARTURES

I let it too close,
that's it.
I felt discomfort at first,
as if doing something indecent,
something not to be done.
I don't know, as if . . .
as if betraying life.

I was mistaken, of course,
as we're all mistaken.

And the more the life
seemed small,
insignificant and offensive
toward anyone believing in it,
the more often I talked with
those who had decided
to end it on their own terms.
I even started to envy them,
in a sense,
for being brave enough
to move on to the other side.
Because the life we live here,
in this place, today,
doesn't really take guts.

This was going through my mind
while waiting for the next train.
Where, when, and how . . .
The only concern I had left.
I'd finally do something
really big,
in this small, messed-up
life of mine.

I'd known for long
it was the fear that
held us here, till the end,
despite everything.
The fear of death. And of life.

I had to stand up against it.
I knew it—once I'd overcome it,
I'd be ready at last.
The more I grew aware of it,
looking it in the eye, the smaller it got.
And I was getting more and more alive.

The hopeless love was replaced by happiness
on realizing I enjoyed a perfect
freedom of choice.

And to make it clear:
I'd not given it up, no way.
Because one cannot afford
such a thing at this place.

Nobody loses hope where I live—
it's not fitting.
It's almost a greater crime
than suicide.

Just as it's no longer fitting
to write poems about despair.
Here, you're simply written off
like old books
or workers from the South,
or they let you be sold,
undersold,
until you're disgusted
by your own life,
and you simply call it a day.

So, I'm going to do the best
I can for myself.
Only this way will I depart proudly,
only this way will I uphold
the little honor I've got left.

With so many self-sufficient,
self-satisfied people inhabiting it,
this world doesn't really need anybody.
They won't even notice I'm gone,
just as they don't notice me here and now.

There's a big sun in me,
shining deeply,
so deeply
only I can see it.
I'll take it with me,
down, underneath the sky.

(*Arrivals, Departures*, 2013)

THE STREET

I spin
in the evening
alone
in the grip of
a clear
memory
pulling
through
the trophy
of dreams
enclosed
in an unclear
message
you ring
the doorbell
that doesn't exist
you wait
below the window
that sleeps
you stir
the conscience
that fades
you desire
the first fight

you didn't finish
for fear
of ending
the friendship.

(*Cut Off from the Sky*, 2018)

MESSI

Once you're gone,
dribbling will be
easier again.
No more
tiki-taka.
The eternity
that nobody wants
to pass off
will only be yours.
The ball
you return at once
is foreign to the character
of the small
and the dumb;
you drag and drag it
until they take it from you.
Crying is the result.
Tiki-taka,
from foot to foot,
without a heart, with a delight
counting money, smiling
from the other side of Barcelona
while taking a shower.
When Messi takes a shot,

the poor slant down
in prayer,
and if he misses it,
it's all the same. This helps.
Those who can, forgive.
The incompetent
only proliferate.
When Messi takes a shot,
you remember
the only thing left
for you to have is a burek,
and it's best
to cheer for one club only,
even if from the second division.
You're just not used to
so many victories.
Only those from the other side
of Barcelona can endure this.
Tiki-taka.
Tiki-taka.
The victory doesn't matter,
only the smile and the pass.
With one touch, or two.

(*Kitula*, 2015)

THE DECK

The aging sailor
remains faithful to
the tremor.

(*Whales Do Not Showboat*, 2000)

THE SEEKER

Drunk from the bus,
terrorized from thinking.
How does the snow smell?
How do you dream?

(*To the Little Boxer*, 1988)

HARA-KIRI

My words
would have
even greater
peace
in Japanese.

(*Cut Off from the Sky*, 2018)

THE DIVAN

I could die,
I could get up.
To know all this
and stay modest.

(*The Divan*, 2006)

THE PRAYER OF THE BUTTERFLY

You open up once,
you close down once.
You use up all the mercy.
And die.

(*Molitev metulja/Gebet des Schmetterlings*, 2014)

A HEART

The memory
of the eternal
life,
waning.

(*Cut Off from the Sky*, 2018)

THE SAMURAI

I'm pierced through.
With the last year's swallows
still flying through me.

(*Cut Off from the Sky*, 2018)

WATER

You'd left.
Gentler than my mercy.
I was waving at you, but I knew
I couldn't return you.
I'm gentle, more and more.
Where are you taking my mercy?

(*To the Little Boxer*, 1988)

THE PATIENCE

I'm ashamed to remember
that you're so tender you're
unable to think about killing.
Remembering your hair
tied by memory,
I'm seized by a peace
only you're familiar with,
who kills with tenderness.

(*To the Little Boxer*, 1988)

HEART II

I'll never get to know the landscape
of your heart.
I'll forever remain a child
staring, failing to comprehend
this love.

(*To the Little Boxer*, 1988)

THE WOLF

Your forest paws travel carefully.
Crossing the sky of the human, stopping
above the abyss of excessive caution.

(*Kitula*, 2015)

SNOW

Believe in snow
and cut yourself up
to make it sting
when it falls.

(*To the Little Boxer*, 1988)

KNIVES

Knives, they sometimes
dream of killing.
Sometimes you wait for them,
calm and naked.

(*To the Little Boxer*, 1988)

THE COURAGE

Someday you'll find a knife
within yourself,
unamazed, because
you'll get to know it at once—
with love.

(*To the Little Boxer*, 1988)

DATES

And I know
you're happy
about failing
to remember the date
you committed hara-kiri.

(*To the Little Boxer*, 1988)

How much time have we got left?
How many snowflakes before the end of time?
Don't ask, buddy.
Just keep falling.

(*Cut Off from the Sky*, 2018)

THE WILL

I'm a crow.
My cry is betraying me.

I'm painless,
tortured.

The will is the cry
of the whipped.

(*Kavala*, 1986)

A POEM

You're a ship.
I'm a silly sailor
looking menacingly
toward your deck.

(*The Wind in the Veins*, 1994)

Omniscience
has its wings
stuck together in the resin
of the pending decay.

(*The Divan*, 2006)

AMERICA

At the end of the sea everything is all right.
A new lace on the left shoe
and a white death on the right one
tired from walking
and getting lost.

(*Kavala*, 1986)

RUSSIANS

Russians never
run away.
It's too far.

(*The Divan*, 2006)

Every step is great,
says the chieftain
walking slowly.

(*Cut Off from the Sky*, 2018)

Born before my mother,
I'd be free.

(*Born Before My Mother I'd Be Free*, fanzine, 1982)

It's hard to look through the eyes
of an animal
reluctant to meet
a human.

(*Cut Off from the Sky*, 2018)

Do you like spruce trees?
I don't know. I've never looked at them
the way spruce trees look at one another.

(*Cut Off from the Sky*, 2018)

GRAY

I don't want to be beautiful.
I don't want to be red.
I don't want to be black.
I don't want to be liked.
Just gray now and then
when my soul aches.

(*Kitula*, 2015)

LORCA

I squeeze you
to the point of bleeding
to the last
stop
of the ambulance
that ceased
to rush
as
it
was
too late.
I'm aware
you'll
soon be
green
again
for good.

(*Cut Off from the Sky*, 2018)

JOBUS

Everybody would gorge,
only you would eat,
slowly and peacefully,
so as not to be devoured.

(*Cut Off from the Sky*, 2018)

Everyone has the right to return from nothingness.

(*Cut Off from the Sky*, 2018)

Sometimes you understand hills
why they are so far.

(*Cut Off from the Sky*, 2018)

Sometimes you go all the way
even if you've lost your way.

(*Cut Off from the Sky*, 2018)

Sometimes you only look once,
thinking you're an anarchist.

(*Cut Off from the Sky*, 2018)

CANADA

A land
where
only
shovels
still have
a deeper
meaning.

(*Cut Off from the Sky*, 2018)

PALESTINE

The world is a skeleton
of an ancient butterfly
not having fallen yet.

(*Kitula*, 2015)

THE PERSPECTIVE

I've hidden
in the bath
and New York
seems
big again.

(*Cut Off from the Sky*, 2018)

Once upon a time,
there was Fidel,
now it's Lidl.[2]

(*Cut Off from the Sky*, 2018)

---

[2] A German global discount supermarket chain that operates over 10,000 stores across Europe and the United States, and since 2007 also in Slovenia.

Where have all the happy people gone?
To buy happiness.

(*Kitula*, 2015)

THE BANANA

Hey, darling,
don't let us
rot
like this banana
we'd neglected
so unanimously.

(*Whales Do Not Showboat*, 2000)

Do get in touch sometime.
At least with your finger up in the sky,
with tenderness in the drawer,
with a crisis in your eyes,
with foolishness
standing in line,
just for me.

(*Arrivals, Departures*, 2013)

Who first raises a doubt,
shall win.
This is also love.

(*The Divan*, 2006)

My sky is not blue
with your eyes red.

(*Arrivals, Departures*, 2013)

I love the spaces in your eyes.

(*Cut Off from the Sky*, 2018)

We looked
at each other
longer than others,
and made it.

(New poetry, 2019)

Power is a façade
you love more
than you love yourself.
Cry it out
down to the wall.

(*Cut Off from the Sky*, 2018)

Give me your hand,
I've taken your heart.

(*Arrivals, Departures*, 2013)

AUTUMN

The ambience is dreadful.
Making the hangman
wink
when the blossom's neck
gets broken.

(*Whales Do Not Showboat*, 2000)

THE ELEPHANT

Only death
is heavier
than your
awkwardness.

(*Elephants Have a Fair Cry*, 2011)

A SEA POEM

My children are gentle.
Even when they can't go
to the seaside, their cry
is deep and blue.

(*Cut Off from the Sky*, 2018)

A TRANSITIONAL POEM

Leave the poetry, son.
There's no money in it
whatsoever.
Let Belarusians
write it,
they've got nothing
to lose anyway.

(*The Divan*, 2006)

Nobody
quarrels anymore.
Only skyscrapers
grow downward.

(*Arrivals, Departures*, 2013)

Sometimes
you jump off
a lower
skyscraper.

(New poetry, 2019)

Sometimes
you think dirty
windows
are the past
you shouldn't
wash away.

(New poetry, 2019)

How do vacant folks
feel during vacation?

(New poetry, 2019)

I like the sun that doesn't change anything.

(*Cut Off from the Sky*, 2018)

You say people are
nothing but morons.
And I, a moron,
believe you
totally
and blindly.

(*Black Jack*, 1994)

AN OUNCE

You've got a river for yourself.
You've got a neighbor for yourself.
Will you kill for an ounce
of unrequited love?
Will you sell out for smooching
with trees that sleep
with everyone?

(Unpublished, 1985)

THE BODY SCENT

The sun has risen behind the Golovec[3] and breathed through
my room.
The state would call it the sun of freedom. With slow and
drowsy gestures
I crawl toward my pants, thinking whether I should eat today
or get fucked-up.

I put on my pants, open the fly, and grab my cock with
my right hand.

With refined movements I wank it up, thinking about the pretty
state official who I gave a wave yesterday,
but who ignored me. Then
I said to myself, you'll be mine, I'll take advantage of you.
And I did
though she didn't feel it.

---

[3] A wooded hill (450 m) close to the center of Ljubljana.

I asked myself if that was love, but hastened to kick myself
cause I'm
revolution and love's a deceptive matter.
I go stand by the window. From there, I observe pretty women.
I wank to every third one.

I'm revolution and love's a deceptive matter.

(*Tribuna* newspaper, front page, 1982)

THE PILGRIMAGE ACROSS THE COUNTRY

I go to school
a grand gala for me
I really feel childish

I stroll among buds turning into blossoms
with every tree being Sava Kovačević[4]
every tree scorched somewhere
over there in Bosnia

I sweat from the heat
but there's no summer anywhere

I don't know
I may be in some German or Russian camp
among my compatriots remembering
their childhood.

(*Tribuna* newspaper, 1982)

---

[4] A Yugoslav revolutionary, a partisan commander, and a national hero killed in Bosnia during World War II.

SHIT

Poets are strongest in the restroom.
Even when shitting, they aren't abandoned by this feeling.
Even when shitting, they're convinced
something magnificent, unique, and inimitable
is coming out of them.
They feel they cannot be withered by oblivion.
When pushing downward like this, they're
smiled at by angels, angels as clean as unused
toilet paper. They find ignorance so dear to their hearts,
so welcome, in those moments of absolute glory,
when no one around them is safe from the rapture
of a prolific poet, this hero of coziness
and easiness. How many times will the moment
have to be repeated that every child takes to their grave,
how many times will he have to suppress his purest fantasies
to finally become the ruler of his own toilet bowl?
For the secret he takes with him every time he sits on it
is the greatest shit of this world.

(*The Divan*, 2006)

Did you hear God take everything from you?
Did you?
If so, tell Him everything.

(*Molitev metulja/Gebet des Schmetterlings*, 2014)

Sometimes you step over a puddle,
thinking you're a snob.

(*Cut Off from the Sky*, 2018)

THE WHITE BLOOD

The wind breathes, my child.
And in this wind, horror breathes
that will never forget us
because we're the wind,
merely a wind that gives
pleasure to this horror.

For we're horrendous,
more horrendous than the wind—
sometimes, on finding
white blood that sleeps,
sleeps in the wind.

Children, joyful children,
offended and angry to the core.
Alive, alive to the core,
unsung and cold.

The killers of the wind
and all the memories
that must not exist
for we were born as seagulls,
not as memories.

I shall equate you, I shall equate you,
nostalgia, I shall equate you
with horror for you to be a seagull,
nameless, harmonious,
more of a human
who remembered
someone
and threw them away
like their own
old uniform.

(*The Angel with Shredded Wings*, 1989)

THE DARK SIDE OF PURE ENERGY

You who screamed toward perfection
and got back your own echo.
No longer do you disturb me.
I know how you filled yourself up,
how you scratched, snooped on
yourself, I know about this.
Because I also sometimes . . .
And the clemency . . .
This is a scandal.
We don't need this,
neither of us.
We know too well it doesn't help,
it only keeps spurring
the sides in the human
that remain unfulfilled.
This is why I'll always
love you
because you're a wolf
that gulped
the same blood,
afraid of your own clemency.
And don't give up

even though your cruelty
makes me sad sometimes.
Gulp, gulp.
Your laughter slowly soothes me.

(*The Angel with Shredded Wings*, 1989)

Kisses are higher
in the rain.

(*Arrivals, Departures*, 2013)

The rhythm sleeps on the tracks.

(*Cut Off from the Sky*, 2018)

It's sad
when one
makes
the sun
just for oneself.

(*Cut Off from the Sky*, 2018)

Sometimes you forget
the friends
who forgot you
ages ago.

(New poetry, 2019)

Sometimes
you hate
those
who never
hate.

(New poetry, 2019)

Sometimes
you clench
the fist
in which
you'd bring
flowers.

(New poetry, 2019)

Sometimes you understand
the birds
that don't sing.

(New poetry, 2019)

I've told you:
Don't share it with people.
For they'll share you,
and become you.

(New poetry, 2019)

WOLVES

They love you all!
They love you all!

They bite,
bite with your teeth,
hungry like you,
scared like you.

They love you all,
they're scared,
they long like you,
wolves.

(*Kavala*, 1986)

THE RAGE

Frightened, rabid dogs tear
at the pale meat,
frightened, they go for it
with their white teeth,
insensitively and bloodlessly,
frightened, they weep,
the body is hungry and void.

Snow 1985

(*Kavala*, 1986)

PALACH

Self-immolation
is a hellish happiness
of overly proud people.

(*Whales Do Not Showboat*, 2000)

The human,
your cruelty
is a bloody river
flowing to the sky.

(*Cut Off from the Sky*, 2018)

One wish, to begin with.
Don't be a friend
because you feel like it
or because your ego feels like it,
equally merciless
toward any individual.
It will be easier for you
to be alone with yourself a bit more . . .
you've got everything there, since forever,
and there's nothing wrong about that . . .

And once you really find nothing else
within yourself, get your oars ready—
there's just one mountain.

(Unpublished, 2016)

THE PEACE

This damn peace.
Roses are falling from the sky.
Heavy white roses
instead of the rain.
Nobody has picked them
from the sky that is the ground.

Who forgets
to recharge the battery
of their cellphone,
can die
instantly,
and rest in peace.

(*The Divan*, 2006)

WANNSEE

Four sausages he's loaded on,
four worries less he's eaten up.
The world is always up there.
While he was eating,
he looked downward,
dipping the discipline in the mustard.
Chewing over his eternal concern:
If only I didn't
run out of bread.

(*The Divan*, 2006)

I'll forget you tomorrow.
Not today.

(*The Divan*, 2006)

Father,
some people
just look up
and already they die with us.

(*Arrivals, Departures*, 2013)

SYLVIA

Resignation is fatal,
their witnesses dead.

(*The Divan*, 2006)

Sometimes you're at peace,
having lost already.

(New poetry, 2019)

AN EPITAPH

Poetry is vulnerable,
but those who write it
haven't been for quite a while.

(*The Divan*, 2006)

A MORNING

A black coffee,
a Black Slave
doesn't get up anymore.

(*Elephants Have a Fair Cry*, 2011)

The silence of a hand
having found itself
in another one.

(*Kitula*, 2015)

PICASSO

Who pilots
the arms of the sky
when the night falls?

(*Kitula*, 2015)

JANUARY

It's spring today.
It got lost.
It can't find the way.
They say it's headed to Germany.

(*Cut Off from the Sky*, 2018)

The rain has given me the roofs back.

(*Cut Off from the Sky*, 2018)

THE APARTMENT

I'll trade a head
and the invisible arm
of a poet
for a three-bedroom
apartment
without walls
and neighbors.
I rent out the naivety
of a child
‚for a blow
of genuine reality
to the chest area.

(*Whales Do Not Showboat*, 2000)

BRDO

A Sunday afternoon.
A moron on a motorcycle
never fast enough for him
is racing toward the end
of the street
his father thoroughly
despises.

(*The Divan*, 2006)

PAINTERS

Hang them
before they
hang themselves.

(*Whales Do Not Showboat*, 2000)

THE NEWSPAPER

He rides past my window
in the morning,
throws me the paper
and kills me
till the next
morning.

(*Kavala*, 1986)

Sometimes you go to the movies
and never come out.

(New poetry, 2019)

HORSES

They stare at the walls,
they stare at the stalls.
Those are their stables.
Come on, my horses!

(*To the Little Boxer*, 1988)

Everything falls
from the sky,
everything
goes into
the ground;
blood and thoughts,
oblivion and fortune,
joy and rivers,
leaves and snow,
wind and escape.
Everything falls from the sky.
And nobody is sorry.
Not even those
waiting
underneath.

(*Arrivals, Departures*, 2013)

ROMMEL

An honorable defeat
burning
sky-high.

(*The Divan*, 2006)

CARRY ME, CHILDREN, ON YOUR HANDS

After the painstaking years
of famine and the weary lying
underneath animal skin.
Across the rivers of blood
flown past
and the bizarre calls
from the darksome woods.
A Sunday route
has been formed,
hot and cluttered
with chaotic dreams
and the songs of the little guys.

Displeased and distrustful
is the gaze of the white dog
on the Sunday stroll.

A crowd of ignorant children
is caressing him across
his gentle eyes and ears.
He's left the beauty,
the terrible bleakness behind.
His teeth are
white and clean.

(*Kavala*, 1986)

THE DUSK

So,
by the evening,
you put on your boots
and tie razors
around your heart,
you apply sweat
to drive away the swan,
to hear the wings
that won't let you sleep.
You hide behind contempt
as if losing it all.
You know it's not that cold
you radiate some black gold.

(*The Wind in the Veins*, 1994)

Elephants have a fair cry.

(*Elephants Have a Fair Cry*, 2006)

I'd met a girl,
a girl with freckles,
she didn't want the freckles,
just gold.

(*Kitula*, 2015)

How do giraffes embrace?

(*Freedom Just Walking*, 1986)

I've met a fox,
a red fox,
he wasn't allowed to be red,
just cunning.

(*Kitula*, 2015)

Borrow my ghost,
clamp it to yourself
and say
you've dressed up the wrong way.
I'll be glad
because your tracksuit
is on inside out.

(*Black Jack*, 1994)

What a danger
you are to yourself.
If you were like this to others,
they wouldn't
like you all that much.

(*Cut Off from the Sky*, 2018)

A PRAYER

To Fernando

A late afternoon.
You cannot write a poem.
It seems you never will.

A late afternoon.
The time when the birds of poetry
get ready for their last song.

When the passing is too shiny
for you to steal its power.

You wrap yourself in the coat
of an impatient emptiness,
under which it's impossible
to resist bestially.

A late afternoon.
And the thickening
the almighty keeps silent about.

The late afternoon
whispers to you gently:
you will forever be scattered
and all your thoughts
will be mine
as they have been
since ever.

(*Whales Do Not Showboat*, 2000)

WHALES

Whales do not showboat.

(*Whales Do Not Showboat*, 2000)

Sometimes
you write
so as not
to kill.

(New poetry, 2019)

Christ doesn't rush.

(New poetry, 2019)

Sometimes you're the snout of a cloud.

(New poetry, 2019)

Esad Babačić was born in 1965 in Ljubljana to a working-class migrant family. After completing his military service in Titograd, Babačić returned to Ljubljana and started studying Slovene language and literature, as well as Southern Slavic languages, in the Faculty of Arts at the University of Ljubljana. His poetry has been translated into many languages and has received several awards, notably the Velenjica–the Cup of Immortality (2014) award for ten years of outstanding poetic work in the twenty-first century.

Andrej Pleterski (b. 1979) is an award-winning literary translator from English, French, and Slovak, and of Slovenian poetry into English and Slovak. In addition to numerous contributions to literary journals and catalogs, he has published more than twenty book-length translations of poetry and prose and compiled four anthologies. He has run the Slovak literary translation workshop organized by the Republic of Slovenia Public Fund for Cultural Activities since 2011.